I0140246

1

THEY HID THE STARS FROM THE EYES OF CHILDREN
Travels of the Mind
Richard Alberto Morillo Guevara-Fabra'

Andrea T. Goldreyer; Editor
Cover Illustration "Dreams" June 2015
by Sonal Phogat Bijnor, Uttar Pradesh, India

Book Cover and Art Design - Lawrence Studio, Inc.
Merrick, New York. USA

SOUTHERN MOUNTAINS PUBLISHING Ltd.
Merrick,New York
southernmountainspublishing@gmail.com

*Published by SOUTHERN MOUNTAINS
PUBLISHING Ltd.*

Merrick, New York. USA

*Library Of Congress Cataloguing- In
Publication Control Number 2017915152*

ISBN 9780986386305

United States of America Copyright 2017

All rights reserved Printed in the United

States of America 2015911062

Corrected first edition

December 2018

Amb l'esperanca eterna que Catalunya sempre viu en total llibertat.

Lovingly dedicated to all my muses; country of birth, adopted land, family and friends. Above all, I respectfully dedicate this book to all Immigrants and Refugees around the globe for their continuing inspiration.

TABLE OF CONTENTS

AN ELEGY FOR AYLAN KURDI

Slowly walk. Don't tilt your head as your feet leave buried footprints on the sand, gently jaunt fearlessly following the threaded steps of millions who preceded you to Europe.

Softly stroll with curious glances lost among granules of sand burned by many suns for endless millennia across the lingering echoes and fading shadows of time.

Proudly walk, not trembling, as with lost dreams in your head attempting to have them dissipate in the hot air of summer.

Amble proudly as unburied newborn turtles with a sense of a scattered pregnant destiny. Hope for a new life while you listen to my drifting rainbows and whispers glancing at your soul.

Ramble coherently with seeds of uncollected human voices washed ashore accompanied by barely blinking eyes during these smuggling frightful times.

Seeds of mangled wreaths pass along the seawater window sills followed by small bodies with eyes closed and vanishing breaths, on the way to having an abbreviated destiny bitten by time, hungry pigeons and naked waves.

Crying mothers forlornly are leaving crystal footprints on a gashed shore used by bantling starfish in an alliance with children's plastic buckets and shovels.

Don't walk the sand beaches of Lesbos or Kios. You might have to walk around my body as this is where I my journey ended, just as my pilgrimage had begun.

My name is Aylan Kurdi. I never played at a beach or owned a beach shovel, yet my last breath was taken aloft this granular shore.

Please remember me as the voice of the living sand murmurs alleviating sounds meant for the forgotten souls seeking asylum through the last earth's window.

October 22, 2016.

I AM JUST A BROWN CHILD

Yes, I am brown. It is not a coincidence that Earth and I share the same skin pigment.

In different shades from rustic poverty to elegant chocolate, our eyes and manes are from sepia to chestnut, from drab colored morning to rich dusk. Our hues are an expression of beautiful and delicate umber.

It is no coincidence that Rubens, Caravaggio and Rembrandt broadly used brown to create a pure, raw and naked chiaroscuro which depicted life's essence and it's luminosity with our soul's pigment.

We are part of a wide visible spectrum. We are red as passion and courage, as yellow as the brilliant corn and sun, as black as the elegant night which foreshadows every morning.

Our skin hue is copper as the healthy skin tone that covers the Earth. We are as visible as the raw tint of our homeland. We are the clay of the Earth.

We are, you and me, all the same. All human, all equal, all magnificent & free, and yet even though we are a blend of the color blood and the sun, we are of low visibility.

We blend with the bright light of the sun.

The same one that blinds you and you...
We are invisible!

October 07, 2014.

A PRAYER AND A SUPPLICATION FROM AN ÉMIGRÉ

We prepare to leave our soil to scavenge this Earth for shelter to furnish warmth to our brethren and family.

I am a refugee from beyond the imaginary bounds set by men native of other lands in other times away from my culture and reality.

Collections of unmoored songs gently skim over the river's white caps, as we sail onward in search of a welcoming land.

Are we far enough from where we no longer hear the stranded lullabies of the ones we left behind? We are sailing past thundering herds of silence and hunger, as well as anthems that are still murmuring over borderline outposts.

At the edge of unnamed crossings hidden behind lost moons, we all struggle not to meet our maker along the road.

Chanting voices crawl along humming parallel soils where mythic songs are ebbing away as we march along to evanescing heart beats of the Earth.

We are trudging along with forgotten masses with pronounceable names. We are wading and plodding over weathered paths in un-pronounceable countries where we are leaving our remains.

On our march for life, sometimes we are harvesting
blessed rainbows, symbols from god. At times the storms
unabashed naked display of fury castigates the soil of our
soul, but not our determination.

We wait for redemption from profound pain after seeing
our children, the infirm and old die before our eyes from
hunger and misery, abandoned from an uncaring god. Are
we not his children too?

Forgive the continuing strain of our un-nourished bones
cradling the innocent darkness, hiding in sheds filled with
groaning dreams ebbing away along
the road where even patience is seen losing its grit to
endure.

Tilted mornings have come and gone without asking for
permission as we've arrived to barbed wire camps where
the masked stench of loneliness
and anxiety is now enclosed in the obliterated life of
unmoored hearts.

Ameliorate our wounded painful flesh, nourish our
empty bellies.
Please give us hope, share your love and compassion.
Help!

December 13, 2015.

LITERARY PRAYER

Heaven's Tyrian tunic with its infinite hidden geometry is embracing our eyes.

Our solitary sermon's sweet words zig-zag to dialogue with loneliness across the threaded fabric of time.

The shape of shadows are angling to displace the wasted light that now belongs to rusted gnawing hours lodged inside the prism of our life's breath.

Our spiritual quintessence is being dealt a life force moment replete with adjuration and an invocation.

Falling silence cascades as autumn leaves mimic disheveled rays of moonlight plunging on the mountain.

Poetical translations have settled in a organically formed urn; crippled, wrinkled from being brined in cryptic moans and wails.

Siblings of storms and impotent prayers are calling all to meditate on the fading light's form and final seminal composition within our transitory chaotic maze.

Has there been rhyme, syntax and even value to our life's endless narrative and composition?

Windswept clouds are huddling under the wings of a prayer.

October 02, 2014.

THE TORRENTIAL RAINS

*A veritable coterie of conscripted vignettes is rolling down
aquiline cliffs.*

*My ashes, accompanied by autumnal rhythms, are
rummaging through time as they await deliverance.*

*Decomposing tulle shadows are drifting as they gaze at
the macabre whirl that is to follow.*

*The morning's music dance is trapping the pulsating light
hovering over my shoulder as my spirit
flinches toward the sky.*

*Winds are broadcasting torrential rains that are washing
my now emptying spirit at the edge of where the
dissipating images are stirring its origins!*

Will blindness follow?

December 09, 2014 – January 11, 2017.

THE QUIET DARKNESS

*I wash my face with the soot of the night right in the
middle of a multitude of humble water mills as they talk
among themselves.*

*Twilight no longer sings. It has fallen into a primitive
trench crouched under a rain delegated and
casted by unknown gods.*

*Clods of vacant hours are enclosed within a lament that is
grouped with images reciting inconsolable muted
soliloquies.*

*Immovable mountains ride on the spine of eternal empty
silence that dialogue with boundless infinite solitude.*

*I will wait for you at the secret forest, next to the empty
window of time, behind the covert and quiet
darkness...where death resides!*

August 12, 2016.

FORGIVEN

Screaming water swallows the fading voices of our forefathers.

The voice clusters behind the ashes that lie on the skin of the soil, as the crossroads where the blue night is washed by the blossoming dew that covers the face of eternity.

It rides on the froth of forgotten voices that twinkle dreams laid to waste.

The Earth swallows the skulls of words that are falling off mountains of breathless birds exposed to melting suns, wilting flowers but still pulsating winters full of life.

The final curtain is eavesdropping on our wounded flesh, to verify our identity, as our mind surrenders to illusions just in front of the iron gates on fire!

July 22, 2016.

THE PRIVATE LIFE OF A SHADOW

You drench the breast of the organic earth with wild light that spreads like molasses. Your energy disrobes before us diffusing the gift of delicate naked perceptible light.

Shattering whirling wings come from the ruptured roots of the sun broken into clusters of intimate wandering dimness.

Shadow, you caress the solid shelter of the penumbra that hides infinite paths of dimness as translucent incipient flowers.

Shadow, you were born out of an angle of rays blocking the rearrangement of lost light speckles surrounding your body.

Gripped by an unsinkable tide of fissuring light spying out of the husk of the moving rays, feeble shadows follow me streaming next to and behind as well as in front of me.

Shadow, I hunger for your company, which arrives in satchels cuffed to the walls and the chestnut earth just before you melt into the wounded night.

Dearest shadow, can you walk, hide and announce rainbows? Can you witness my homecoming steeped and wading in nostalgia beyond the threshold of incoherent patches of squalls riding on the vertebras of an everlasting moon?

Hidden snuggled tumult is riding on top of a pond reflecting an umbra of stars residing and dancing on its skin.

The lost shadow is walking with his half-brother silence,
jaunting hand in hand with your step-dad death...
A perennial agitated shadow of Egyptian dusk is putting a
dull shovel to a raging Earth looking for dignified light as
well as my dreams before they sleep in a cauldron!

November 10, 2016.

DRAWING STRENGTH FROM JULIETA'S DREAMS

You chased fading whispers in the chiaroscuro shadows where eternal spring slept among the ruins giving birth inside your heart.

Your dreams floated away on beds of motionless domestic light and withering battered taunting stars washed by forgotten tears.

You travelled with eyeless faith in the direction of where ashes had fallen from a burning meteor as well as singed wings of birds which came too close to the sun. Now your chimeras, in the shape of idle glass fragments, are flying back to the heavens to accompany your lifeless diluted body.

Don't despair my loving Julieta, for your dreams and legacy will continue within the realm of our young healthy hearts to be dispersed out among the forthcoming generations in whose body your yearnings and longings will live forever.

Now stricken hearts in the brink of sorrow are spawning new dreams drawn from your strength, determination and unwavering will.

Your virtues live on in the altars and hymns that belong to your soul as part of new songs in the form of lullabies.

Chants are sung to the heavens and unstained dawns that will illuminate our Moirai replete with weightless undisturbed typhlotic stones.

August 22, 1991.

AND THE WILLOWS WILL WEEP

As my eyes shifted behind the branches, I hunched and shivered as my startled eyes shrunk to the point where I could barely see.

Your figure, partnering with the whispering winds, palpitated along with the Earth as a stethoscope to the chest's left ventricle.

Your indistinguishable aroma choreographed itself towards me intertwining with the accumulated seeds of lost loves and cascading weeping willow leaves that traveled and descended past the ignominious barren latitudes in search of water.

Let's create a scriptural love enshrouded by the face and trunk of a weeping willow and the enchanted grasslands living on the edges of the planet.

Let's cement our visceral narrative by chaining it to its torso... before the tree cries in passing contempt and deliverance bypass the psalms.

I'll kiss you before I quench my prayers so they won't be imprisoned inside the beautiful bark of a weeping willow.

Do we need Moses to bring us some flowers?
Do we need redemption?

March 07, 2014.

ANONYMOUS BIRDS

A bird's life is distilled before surrendering to the night imbedded in the crepuscule of un-occupied inherited tribal lands. The outcasts of drunken winds are riding on veins of winding topsoil summoning the echoes of ancestral spirits ushering in postcards from beyond.

Transcendent disarmed birds, under the pseudonym of discrepant tree shadows, are submitting their counsel to adrift echoes of ravaged voices emanating from epistles read to absent crumbling hearts.

Unclaimed birds are riding on the gaunt lights boring into the bare breasted porches filled with shimmering stained glass images in the skyline. They reside amidst the spangled grasses clasping on to the prophetic scripture lands.

Birds with pseudonyms are persistently flying over unquenched fire smoke in autumn forests, lit by the roadside fires and lanterns that live in inert existential celibate cities.

Sequels to nameless birds' lives are being launched towards southern sunset roads where trolleys are running alongside phantom transformative byways that surrender to new flight paths.

Out of a hermit's ruins, I stumble out with the birds flocking unrestrained, as they hoist incubated love, meditation and the swarming stream glow of peace.

February 21, 2014.

AS THE NIGHT BLOOMS

In the far flung dismembered fields of time, the eyes of gloom live.

The wheels sparkle as they strike the soil rushing through gardens of fire marching out of caged habitats.

The night blooms borrowing tar cinder and soot from the passing hours heading toward borrowed rivers and feathers of time - which are heckling the coming emerging light.

Soledad is consorting with coughing tunes that   are asleep in our trachea.

The night blooms inside temples of doom. Time has no bounds. The Earth's journey is finite, not as our heartbeats delivering radiant energy on this coherent ancient journey, even as the night's buds are flourishing

June 02, 2017.

MEMORIES

I am a shepherd of delicate fermented memories that revolve around fertile orchards enclosed inside my mind. I own the shadows with no name that journey in the direction of sepulchers leaning on daybreak dissipating in canyons masking as furrows!

September 07, 2017

INNOCENCE

I've plucked the feathers of innocent bronze birds on my roads of wrath and indiscipline.

Spring still danced as I fondly greeted the morning leaving its snug creaking pier.

I inhabited winter brooks before you came with those splendid innocent eyes looking at me and calling me Dad.

I had some treacherous landings before you signed on to my chaotic world.

It was drizzling in my campfire that by now was purged of warming fires and splintered wood.

I was at the mercy of ripened sorrow just as your voice recited my name with joy which suddenly changed from Richard to Daddy.

To the world and to you, I still have no name other than Dad.
Can I howl my new name in the forest?

December 20, 1984.

BATTERED CHILDHOOD

Beneath the dark streets in the sky, I walk endlessly wandering on my tender feet as my soul empties itself out of its drenched and deferred dreams.

I sail pass the foundry from where they attempt to shape me the way they want, where I am smeared by a collective philosophy that engenders my desire for independence of thought and reasoning.

As my small figure stains the night, I continue to ambulate past the frosty weather whipping my skin, as well as my fragile mind in search of a destination which leads me back to the loving shelter of Mom who was forced to leave our homeland.

My unending garden of pain is ameliorated only by constant movement, as I am in the process of harvesting water from river dreams furrowed by lost winds in my imagination.

I am getting tired, but nevertheless I must continue, even if I need to stride on my knees on these asphalt gardens.

I must continue beyond my capacity towards my destiny. What do I know? I am only 9 years old. I'll keep walking to discover, learn and suffer in the process of nourishing my heart.

Perhaps one day I'll share and converse with everyone about my travails and forays into a cruel and difficult world.

The stars in the sky are aligning themselves to guide me home.
My brightest star is south. The sun is almost sapping the darkness out of the heavens.
The sunlight is combing the back of my heart.
It is time to go home!

April 09, 2014.

THE SOUND OF A CHILD'S VOICE

*The sound of your voice takes me to faraway lands where I
ride with a smile on the beams of light that emanate from
your credulous eyes.*

*I close my eyes so as to travel to the land of cotton candy,
circuses, the fat lady, clowns, sorcerers, magicians
and lions.*

*For a time, we shared our days on the ghosts of early
spring and summer accompanied by chromatic swirls of
laughter and joy that ride on mythical carousels
in the tenement of our voyage.*

*The echoes of your voice brought inner chaste notions of
inherent curiosity and laughter. These reverberations
bounced around my walls from where they climbed from
my feet to my heart.*

*In the skin of infinity, a little more than a few centuries, I
find myself searching for the re-assuring innocent sound
that scorched my landscape with a wink and a smile.*

*I am still anchored to the footsteps of your voice's whisper
that drips from your backpack.*

Where have you gone?

May 01, 2015.

EVEN THE NIGHT HAS EYES

*My awakened whispering bones nestled in the mid-night
of our journey devour the light, while blooming within
silence, time inexorably dissipates into the body
of the hollow earth.*

April 01, 2011

DO I EXIST?

*My identity submerged itself under the   saddle of your
history.*

*My identity hides in the branches of the silhouettes of
labyrinths that pursue my lisping silence.*

*Is my existence under arrest?
I harbor myself in between the dismantled
structure of your spoken for heart umbrella.*

Does my essence exist?

April 30, 2013.

RAW WOUNDS

There are cracks in the sky through which the wounds of my soul enter between the ruts of rocks of a blue-less sky.

Some ulcers are only crystalline spots that dance before the mirror that reflects my scars. Others reflect bonfires that hide my passion, pain and wild savage raw wound.

Condensed droplets of water wash my bones as well as my blood offerings that parade in the direction of your presence.

There are no distances and borders that separate my eyes and my sense of smell from your path which is already covered by flower petals and shavings.

I'm waiting to see you making my gash bleed just before I dialogue with the guardians of the sky.

At noon, while my pain is having a siesta, my raw agony is buried in the half-light of a stretch where my bruises burn themselves inside handfuls of hidden veins.

My grief travels within and over ridges that journey to constellations where my lacerations miraculously disappear as paramours of meteorites.

June 01, 201

FAINT VOICES

Our hearts' faint echoes and ambling voices can still climb the hills where we use to hold hands. We can't ascend with the verve and fortitude that distinguished our youth and flaw-less middle age, yet we manage nonetheless.

We can still harness the timber of our voices sketched in our pupils, as we grieve for the strength and time wasted frolicking in celebrations that rode on the squalls of attenuated realities.

For now, we swallow the flashes of the extended dark nights, slipping and slithering, riding on the waves of the early hours tattooed on the rails of unknown rivers of blood squalls.

Our voices are hitching a ride inside our fragmented veins, affected by the withering winds that prowl our garden's terrace.

The hands of time are crawling along as a steady trawler reclining over sweet waters, riding on the swells that move under the moon's rays guiding us through dust storms on our way to convalesce behind a rigid labyrinth's anagogic fractured rainbows.

Resplendent youth still fills our young hearts, but the skeleton's conflict with gravity continues. It is still prone to the vicissitudes of the welded history between our enduring soul and our passion to continue to work on the land.

Our account in the pursuit of happiness is careening toward not so subtle and as of yet undiscovered lands, lands where we will share our space with rusted ghosts who have already gone through a fundamental transubstantiation.

Our forlorn enduring voices attest to the gripping contempt that pushes the limits of truth, until our bones are no longer angry and in pain.

Our faint voices are scattering. Where does our history begin?

April 15, 2015

MOTHER

As the voice of the dawn, your evocative soothing warm rain always bathed me with joy, but because you are no longer here a stream fills my eyes with vacant glances, laments and endless meditation.

Mother, spider webs of cannibalized voices hunt to scream at me, but I no longer have ears.

Through time-travel, you bring forth a blistering array of embryonic rays that will illuminate my path through eternal unbroken nights. Your cradling limbs help me sidestep the shunned snarling woven sunsets that await us all.

Under your guidance I apprenticed from love to sorrow, and now that I have mastered both the craft of living and suffering, I am walking in a flower garden adrift the blooming undiscovered roads that bifurcate in this not long enough path of our existence.

Life is full of defiant inconsistencies along with innumerable inner monologues that just confuse our senses and soul.

Please don't let go of my hand yet. Take me in the direction of never ending love.

Let me rest on your window sill where I can still nest when the raw glacial cold violent air encroach my doomed brittle bones
May 31, 1966 – July 04, 1991.

WADING IN SHALLOW RIVERS

My days began gazing at and embracing the continuous caged rains which were unleashed and mandated by unknown gods who always abandon the forgotten.

Since I was made of clay, I was a bit trepidatious because of the rain announcing itself via uttering groans, as lost letters losing their grip from sentences written on cumulus clouds that always latch on to them.

Raindrops succumbed to the gravitational pull of the Earth as it passed through a glass door leading to the candled orange groves and cornfields caressing my wedded land.

The untamed skies were set ablaze by the loosing grasp of the raindrops that now walk past the blinking plasticity and the passive malleability of the city.

The constant stream poured into the unblinking street rivers cuddling all inhabitants with its sorcery.

The unaccounted water is slowing my pace, making me feel as though I am trudging with leg irons.

I rise from the streets and leap onward in search of respite from the rains. I want a truce with Mother Earth as I continue to archive life's lessons in my expiating vitreous joints.

We are wading in shallow waters, as we archive life's lessons in our brittle bones.
The endless journey must continue even in sodden soil.

March 01, 2001 -March 14, 2017.

RIVERS IN SILENCE

*I pulled up my anchor away from the forgotten river
bedrock where the misty fog rose to cross cities in silence,
up and over the spinal cord of the sky to where pawnshops
for desolate lost souls are open for business.*

*Souls that up 'til now have been hiding inside raindrops,
landing on top of river foam water to conjugate as
conjunctions between shadows and stuttered movement
skimming over still un-awakened water.*

*Can we rescue our soul from lonesomeness at the edge of
our pierced world? We are encircled in villages with
windmills to dream along with souls that crawl and paddle
amid raindrops to reach their destination.*

*Humanity is guided from entangled gardens and waterless
borders with no stairways to lead us out to our inherited
dreams, from where we can fly as sparrows across river
basins carrying our dreams in a quiver.*

*We glide above a fortress that unleashes an army of naked
voices that swarm on motes filled with unvarnished and
doomed mourning that orbits over inherited pain and
loneliness.*

*Moonlight peels away from fluttering persistent songs
that descend toward the pathway of unflattering
remembrances of white invisible muted wafting corpses.*

*Nights are full of breathless ghost trails leading to a
courtyard of memories and decaying footprints, dislocated
and squandered at the battle front with moonlights that
surrender to oblivion.*

I gather the light on the perimeter of the geography of angst through the empty streets of midday that gashes the beckoned shadows traversing the breasts of the meadow, as well as moons and aging forlorn nights that flock to my salvation.

Blind echoes of garden relics are plowing over the light, touching the threshold of freedom and self-revelation washed in glitter.

Silent rivers at the edge of our scorched Earth are encircling the light whose beckoning is minting autumnal tattered moons.

I write my name on drifting dust chasing slumbering unborn ice mornings that are dancing on rivers in silence.

May 31, 2016

I WAS CRADLED BY THE WHIMS OF FORTUNATE WINDS

We first saw each other as the twilight settled under the horizon. Our glances sent each other's life story as their chimeras nested along with the echoes of words dreamt inside a bird's feathered brain. I was cradled by the land and its universe, where in a nest I put echoes of my thoughts amid those dreams of condors flying through the rough-hewn twilights.

Under peaceful and gleaming horizons next to engaged wooden wheels, I psychoanalyzed the dreams of birds who had been fetch outside my window of time by the whim of fortunate winds.

In this Arcadian landscape, both of our dreams danced together as sole witnesses of the gospel truth about our vicissitudes and joys of times gone by.

Bird's dreams attested to the ever fleeting nature of events and terms of our lives, which were as languishing Harmattans that assaulted the dreams and aspirations in our life.

The winds stood as transportation to forgotten dances under the cedars, while doves flew in an amber sky as sole onlookers. The whim of lost winds jostled the birds as they congregated just before flying toward a landing next to Freud's couch. What were they thinking?

Should we continue to attempt to analyze birds' dreams, or focus on our own? They might be talking about us. Until we meet again in the forever heavens!

May 07, 2009.

CRAWLING THE HEIGHTS

*As I silently gaze at the azure, distant suns are wrestling
with dusk and the bell's rumble is rising toward the carved
sky with unannounced twilight rays.*

*They are beckoning the plume thistle and the aster flowers
in spring as the everlasting Earth's wrapping
flourishes before the heavens!*

*Out of the Earth's chamber, peace rises as an effigy of the
moon encapsulating the bare steel. The naked brick
and still porous wet mortar ogles at the city creeping
upwards.*

*Unleavened silence in communion with undocumented
time crawls to awaken the desert with its fragmentary
barren and hostile slivers of unprotected life.*

*Spellbinding cavalcades are carrying our sighs and gasps
hunting apocryphal winds, even those that are making our
sails unfurl between the naked waves.*

*We crawl toward the heights of the heavens away from
untied man made valleys where we harbor the light within
our solitary soul.*

*Our heart is being buried under a hidden wreath among
the unknown lands and the savage rains coming down
from the heavens.*

*Up in the mountain, the hermit's mood is compelling the
smoke to rise, to bore the sky in disarray from infidelity
and tears as destiny hangs precariously from its apex.*

Sea shell shape clouds, among silhouettes of gravediggers,

are redeeming the execution of the nocturnal sadness
which finally crawl the height of the Earth and our spirit!

June 01, 2017.

COLLECTED RIVER NARRATIVE

In a new birthed night, we began yarning lullabies in barns where birds, owls, and geese shared their home with swarms of fireflies.

The quiet limping turbulent voice echoes are part of the dissipating throngs of our narrative chatting with river water.

The transitory journey is in danger of being drowned in the twitching fog of blind ashen history.

Pioneering zeal perilously teeters from the self-contained abyss that envisions un-translatable idioms flowing on budding currents.

A river's uncollected love sonnets are hiding behind sculpted ancestral river stones.

Translated shadows without a biography or even exploratory reflection have stationed their metaphoric lurking presence in the anatomy of unyielding history.

Unknown rivers are swept to metamorphose into an incarcerated paragraph in our autumnal humble borrowed libretto.

September 26, 2016.

THE NEFARIOUS WEATHER

Distant calls haunt my soul inside my corporeal warehouse. They are unconvincing as iniquitous revelations and faithful reality halted from reaching the sounds of the unaltered Earth's breath.

The vanishing light is moving away before being exhumed by time inside a nefarious structure sequestered under the last highway's candle light lumen.

We are all marching towards intertwining roads leading to obscured ghettoes and contradictory sorrows that do not offer a way out of this ruined forest and inhospitable opprobrious weather!

*We live in a monastery full of spirits encouraging us not to relinquish peace and quietude, even as we journey through the valley of fear and uncertainty, flashing unrecognizable pierced water carvings forged
in the sky!*

August 12, 2016.

A JOURNEY

I left your jagged shore amid the threshold of a storm.

I felt that I would be safe even though the pulse of these waters were hard to decipher.

They were as hard to decode as my breathing through a crystal skeleton, as hard as naked Jungian dreams that exist as mere abbreviations for your unknown name.

One day I will hand you a fist full of salt, even if just to cover your life lines, vague shadows of a life adrift in silence.

March 06, 1984.

ON GETTING OLD

*I am debilitated, ancient as the wall of China, I hope
venerable. if I am lucky, I'll be as clay drying in the sun
behind the steeples and sun-dried fields from where ghosts
depart after having lost a race by a half step to the winds.*

*I am not tired of seeing my face-lines, only of water lines
that inexorably move up in an attempt to drown me in
an ocean of despair and doubt.*

*I always have dreams inherent in spring and walk on
steppes that hasten to protect me from the cold just as the
song feed the gourd when fall and winter dismount on
Earth.*

*The scent of foot soldiers and their boots carrying my
coffin are spawning a definition about disconnected coves.
They have been accelerated, provoked by encoded
messages endemic to hidden in harbors where our wounds
continue to be trodden before being interred with our
bones still alive.*

*Archived in my bones are the disintegrating events at the
swirling edges of history which have been erased by the
singular fervor of the lights gathering together
in a nihilistic wreck.*

*We have evolved past apocalyptic collages that depict the
fading sparkling eyes that can no longer blink.*

*The monoliths are recording the turbulent dreams
migrating towards our last earthly journey. Even the caged
birds are making one-winged signals indicating unbridled
freedom as un-rehearsed grief still crawls in my veins.*

Drakes have escaped from the water in an attempt to console us by making solitary sounds that stroll among fading flowers while walking navigable roads that open to new worlds.

Don't worry. There is no end in the horizon yet, no one at the pulpit to witness the remnants of our despair!

March 12, 2016.

DOWN MY SECRET STREETS

*I contemplate the evidence after collecting sediment from
the best and wretched seasons that live within my husk, on
an undisclosed street that lives under a grinding siege.*

*The altered flowing remote sands on my shared watch are
quietly stirring the oscillating dance forged on the
fluttering echoes hanging on the ancient branches of my
anatomy. The murmurs of silence are lashing my
remembrances with original austere illusions inside
my soul's glens.*

*Under the timeless bough that bifurcates around the
secret willows, my neglected body navigates in woodlands
and malleable trails brimming with blossoms of passing
lingering shadows.*

*Forgotten promises are separating themselves out of the
inlaid translations that are scattered as timeworn
wreathed shrines at the edge of the postcards in my
fizzling remembrances.*

*As I walk down my secret streets, hollow poetic winds
dance brimming with newly minted inspirations
dislodged from the wrinkles on my face.*

*Tender darkness is seeking wingless illusions snaking out
rampant flares smoldering in solitude, while embracing me
on my secret street where I live in blind somber anguish I
am but a flightless bird wreathing the top of the hourglass
in cadence with the echoes of the night
bursting through the windowsill of my secret streets.*

August 22, 2017.

ELEMENTAL/ FINAL STRUGGLE

*I throw my ashes as kindling to a pyre that serves as a
besieged lighthouse in the purlieu of an island
that is home to fugitive and forsaken souls.*

*I stain the silence with my whispered screams as escaped
water from a Wadi.*

*Ancient skin-dust dances away from our decaying bodies
as though yielding to the last line in the psalms.*

*Defiant ravaged incantations and digestive byproducts of
our life mingle with disintegrated matter in the elemental
struggle for life and spirit.*

*My ashes 'lightscapes' out of the pyre through primitive
layers of clay, quivering sedimentary embers and
prophecies that connect me with the rest of all
fossils in this evolutionary geography.*

*I've slept for a few thousand years. I repose in a tranquil
and serene golden excavated setting where I am reborn as
an archeological artifact ready to wander.*

*I am clothed in burlap and riding a wheelbarrow...
Someone is about to explore my inner anthropology.*

Am I back with the living?

I think I'll consult with my dream!

June 12, 2014.

A BRIEF JOURNEY AT THE CROSSFIRES OF MY CHILDHOOD

The first lines of this narrative begin, as it continues with a complete disregard for any type of enclosures, corporeal as well psychological.

My street life began at age eight after my Mother moved to the USA. I found myself eager to advance with total naïveté and an indifference to dialogue with danger. I ran, skipped and walked unabashedly without any concern to my vulnerability.

I reluctantly claimed the streets to be mine. They were a symbol of my freedom. There were no signposts to discourage my swashbuckling leap of faith into the unknown.

The first indications of winter did not discourage me from endlessly leaving my footprints all across my native city from the now forgotten forests of the northwest as well the steep ravines of the east.

They are now urban developments that seem to have destroyed the inherited colonial natural beauty of what was meant to last for generations.

It was on these streets that I forged my young heart by bonding with the street urchins to whom these alleys and urban byways belonged to. In these alleys, I learned the "basic sandwich," a mix of mud with a little water for consistency wrapped with a slice of stale bread. They said it was a way to fool the stomach into thinking it was full. They called it 'hunger cauterize'.

The rest of our food came when we 'visited' fruit markets where because of my rather noble, guiltless look,

*I was used as a decoy distracting the shop owner,
engaging her in a conversation by begging for a free pear
while my acquaintances 'borrowed some fruit.'*

*When in my quiet moments, during interminable edgeless
nights sleeping under a park bench, my brain, earth and
body recoiled with hidden doubts about my day's
activities. I told myself that it was just forecasted fate and
survival.*

*By this time, I already felt that my prayers had been
kidnapped. My behavior was nothing more than transient
inconformity.*

*It was elliptically assembled wounded reality, confused
with a narrative of an unhappy child dreaming, embraced
by the shawl of the evening which was not easily receding.*

*As far as I was concerned, I was just trying to find my
Mother. I was just longing to dialogue with the good Earth
or my sisters and brothers who had been hiding under
unnecessary branches.*

*I was lost under the intense surveillance of the neglected
cross fires of weathered time and by the remnants
of inconformity.*

*Intersecting blazes and the recruited rain are wounding my
struggling heart bidding to wash my footprints which were
a bastion of courage, innocence and a noble desperate
spirit.*

May 31, 1968 - September 27, 2003.

RECLUSIVE SUNRISE

I saw the next reclusive sunrise whisper a rhapsody in a dialect that only your heart could comprehend.

It wanted to curl in your heart. It wanted to craft exalted hymns to the joyous remembrances, to the deep profound love that once bloomed in your atrial affectionate dwelling.

You know I was the bricklayer that once built a love palace to our dreams. Now I'm perched on the left side of the moon attempting to resurrect and cradle our now charred voices so we can sing together once more.

There's still time to sing a duet of allusive songs. I swear to you they will not be sung A cappella for the moon's humming distant roar will be accompanying us.

Let's find a roundabout in the sky. Let's peel the layers of frozen rubble, where you hide the remnants of our love.

Let's borrow the book of hope from my dream shelf, before it fades and degrades. Let's wag the tail of time.

Don't skip and jump over my illusion. Let's retrace our dreams. Let's go inside a time capsule full of history, ardor and peace.

Please let's go on!

January 09, 1998 – October 23, 2014.

SLAVERY/SAILING THROUGH

My heart sailed on vessels that followed a torrent of echoes taking me to another dimension by cutting through the space between the clouds and drifting rainbows, where I clutched onto the light yearning for freedom.

I took this vessel ride on a galleon meant to travel toward ancient sea harbors, where I joined with boundless never ending caravans of lost souls fervently yearning to escape from the hypnotic grasp of darkness.

My heart was throbbing and wanted to burst like an overflowing levee. My blood was ready to escape from my body to feed vines of roses and discarded bones just as the twilight rung its bells.

My muffled voice wanted to give way to rising suns, humming lullabies in the midst of spring gardens before the mantle of night would envelop all flowers and rags taken from my dwindling wardrobe.

Breaking branches, snow storms, darkness and ghosts strike me all the way to my eyelashes, enough to awake me to a broken reality. Where is my god and my pregnant stars? My lost rusted horizon is not guiding me to freedom.

Crying times hurl my sleep in the swarm of lacerated nights torn asunder and crumbling until we awake holding leg, neck and wrist irons, silent relics, burnt ashes and a broken heart.

Yet, I continue because hope and dreams of liberty inspire my spirit born free under all the existing latitude of my soul.
My progeny one day will prance on top of unbound soil

where I will rest undisturbed in their liberated land for Aeon.

September 27, 1997.

THIS LAND WHERE WE PLOUGH

In this land, we plant olives, grapes and wheat amidst brooks, thistle, moss and raw dandelions. In this terrestrial land of war, battles, rain and broken mended hearts, we witness solemn nights when we cultivate our dreams.

In this terrain of pantheons, closed eyes and howling drops of acid rain, sounds of copper, platinum and ugly fleshed uranium reverberate and radiate before us.

These cultivated emerging roots speak to us all. They sprout as grains on Earth as the warmth of the sun heats the layers of clay that hides our identity in its bosom.

Salvation trumpets spill as timeworn melted limbs of painted cliffs unraveling by the wayside of this land wrapped in infinity.

It is on this patch of earth that we love and where we grow only at the speed of our child's dreams coming to fruition as well as the pace of a broken down carousel with a faceless giraffe, one legged horse and crying clown.

On this land we plant with our bare hands and lacerated feet as well as hearts in pain. We hope that this land will help us end poverty, hunger and mend our broken hearts.

From this land, we honor and treasure each glimpse into new horizons of frankincense, myrrh, laughter, peace and understanding. We share this globe with the secrets and mythology of all men and women in the name of peace, love and sharing.

August 03, 2014.

A REPORTAGE

As images vacillate to ponder their undocumented existence, life lines intermingle with time propagating its own existence.

At the altar to the sun, sun light is being kidnapped by the rouge of the moonlight, as stacks of shadows neatly announce their presence by embroidering a dusky voice.

The radiant umbra of the moon chronicles its presence and ours with a dance at the cadence of tremors inside our adrift clenched nocturnal retinas...

Liquid bluffs are melting, forming a communion with the brittle bruised skin of a weeping globe while we plough our hoarse earth.

May 01, 2016.

THE MOUNTAINS, MY MOUNTAINS

The hills greeted me with a twinkle of breezes as I
transversed the streets of the city whose iconic landscapes
were several hundred years in the making. They were
sharing their spattered shrills and unparalleled horizon
with my soul.

I walked these streets endlessly looking to meet the
shaman of the mountains, who would dip and immerse me
in the millennial history hemmed in by the bluff and
precipices of its enveloping narrative.

The clouds' movement danced naked in and around my
mountain, creating a fear that fed the gallop and
lengthened the stride in the chambers of my heart on its
journey toward your fountain.

The night's tangled shadows peddled and shared its scant
light with me, as fragmented croaking voices of
tenants living in ravines of armored silence.

The beating stars reposed and dreamt of meteors in the
lashing heavens. They helped to un-clot the veins of
my blinded eyes starving to ensnare the limpest of
lights to help me scan and chronicle the future.

A coffin of hums and restless voices are flying toward the
grave of the moon, where encrypted memos are breaking
the vow of silence and celibacy.

The abstract plumage of firewood glow is flying on wings
of spattered rainbows and waterwheels of sounds and
inter-connective hums in its sequenced spectrum.

My restless soul is binging on the flickering rays devouring

the night as I scan the glimpses of unattended history
cohabiting in the well found in the alcoves of
the heart of these mountains.

July 01, 1998 - August 22, 2001.

THE ESSENCE OF MY CITIZENSHIP

*Its essence exists in the nourishing resolve and constancy
of singular cries from the heart on behalf of all peoples,
lands and humanity with unforgiving liberty.*

*The attributes of my citizenship do not extend to the realm
of nationalism, but in the raw vaults of self-determination
where the only possibility is to live, prosper and
find redemption.*

*My citizenship doesn't yield to the drought of the soul, but
to the splendor of the free soul billowing out, so as to
claim that we all belong to the whole of one land without
borders.*

*The discovery of new brotherhoods of arpeggios are being
stitched and created by albatrosses. They are created by
clans of feeble reflections about different births of cryptic
protagonists seeking temptations in departed gazes lost in
threads of enigmas.*

*Rotating thorns are being unleashed upon my corporeal
matter as a wagon wheel in transit on the Oregon trail,
the whimper of fortified unanchored landscapes.*

*Intangible universes are collapsing as they rattle toward
exiles inside cauldrons of exhausted dreams secretly
distancing from the hem of my marrow.*

*New moons are brandishing telepathic interviews with
disengaged characters, unknown organic winds tasked
with delivering my identity across new frontiers before my
extinction.*

Rented masks are covering my many faces as I attempt to decipher where I belong before the night burns beneath the flesh of the Earth.

I shudder to think how I forgot the true origins of my soul. It rests beyond the boundaries of the half moons of my open canvass.

Call me an idealist!

July 04, 2016.

GHOSTS OF RIVER SHADOWS

We walk past gentle pillars of dark shadows and water,
past confused dreams inhaling iridescent mutant moons
hidden under the riverside's gravel cohabiting quietly with
my well worn heart.

Rustling leaves embrace the night river waves in the
middle of the perishing night's firmament. The river
shadows are unraveling before riding away on
alabaster sailing froth.

The shroud is unlacing itself from the fading furrows of the
rill. The specter of phantom river dwellers is being
orchestrated by the coming tides.

Conversations with migrating undocumented intruders are
taking place amid evaporating river shadows.

The shore's shadow is sitting on broken foam branches
interred under dusk's roots, sitting alongside a
gravestone's quilt while rainsqualls gaze from the river!

March 29, 2017.

I AM A PAWNBROKER IN THE FIRMAMENT

I ride and wander through the night sky's carousel thirsty, naked and shivering; wrapped in clouds, where the stars intermittently come out to get a glimpse of you.

I've travelled from shore to shore within the confines of this cathedral in the sky amid the currents in this sea of clouds that sing your name.

I travel lending not money but hearts and smiles in between stars that from the distance look like bits of broken mirrors.

I am the pawnbroker in this lake of shadows where I archive our suffering pain, blindly tumbling on ledges of roads that pierce the night.

The skies launch impregnable dreams that conceal the forged oasis that flower in the riverside of the cosmos.

I am the pawnbroker in a firmament which is still beneath earthly tender soil lit by street lamps that mimic the sun!

November 28, 2015.

I ONCE WAS A HUMMINGBIRD

We wreathed lagoons inside nests that were woven by
sacred fires plus hand me down fabric left by the forest
and tidbits of catalogued time and its history.

Out of ashes, bark and shredded leaves threaded with silk,
we made my home perched in the land among the orchids,
lilies and bromeliads.

Out of the emerging memory of the life of the forest, we
nourished ourselves with sacred honey that nature
provided. The temporal crystal borders of the darken sun
of centuries still endure among the intolerant screams
that threatened me like the serpents and arrows of
natives in their grey landscape.

Nevertheless, I prospered before the mirror snatched my
reflections in a jade cage inquiring about my
feathered shadow.

With face signals and whistles to each other, I leaped with
my peers to alleys filled with naked dreams of free lands to
evade our infinite annihilation.

In a whirlwind, we were swept by currents to unknown
sanctuaries hidden by time behind thunder and rain that
did not thwart our demise.

Now swarming silence clothes my unimaginable downpour
of painful echoes, stench and death.
I once was a hummingbird...
May 07, 2012- May 01, 2017.

SILENCE CROSSES BARRIERS

With urgency I smile overwhelmed before biting the earth.
At this stage, I bear witness that these doors open and
close in one direction.

As silence travels, there is a perfume of white flowers that
anguishes the soul!

Even on a heron's wounded wings, quiet crosses the
barrier's twilight in random directions, just as the night's
hush forms a chain of memories that run peacefully
forward, as hidden voices that crawl on
all cardinal points.

The emblem of silence battles with hidden winters that
cross distances toward grasslands full of eternal suns.

Silence conveys the rungs hidden in meadows of horizons
and chasms in constellations of hush and pain.

I hope that the cartilage and bones of infinity do not run
aground on my beaches at dusk.

I hear the soothing sound of your soul on my pillow, where
a drizzle of gazes clears my heartache.

I am not superstitious, but to make sure that these
sparkling glares remain,
I'll take a piece of silence as a charm in my pocket.

I continue to bathe in streams of peace, with tiers
of nameless winds hauling your silent smile throughout all
seasons.

December 31, 2012.

THE WHITE HELMETS

*To you my dear heroes, to your lingering pledge,
commitment and passion for others lost and teetering in
humanity's peril, I salute you.*

*To you that soar above the finely honed fissured stained
glass that hold hope, beauty and nostalgia in its elevated
naked metaphors carved by sunlight, I honor you.*

*The spume and gales of firebombs chime eternity as you
roll in, not cowering, but heroically scooping life's marrow
out of inlets of destruction and wind struck dwellings.*

*You dig a handful of summer river willows as the mistral
briefly dozes.*

*Your wounded skin clatters as it chatters earnestly with
interrupted blood lines registering a child's pulse to warm
and clothe the pain.*

*The breast of the morning is opening its bosom over the
bloody fields filled with dust, carnage and massacre...
White helmets, you are already harvesting life, while
frustrating and reprimanding death
and obliteration to stay away.*

*You are lifting the curtains of darkness. You are bringing
hope and inspiring our hearts, providing rescue for the
flesh of our soul's existence. Please go on. Proceed!*

October 01, 2015.

SELF-PORTRAIT

*Amidst the mismatched voices that surround me, I bemoan
and lament your absence in my unfinished childhood.*

*The forfeited evidence of your presence was left as treads
on the steps of the enfeebled church as
I walked on the margins of spring.*

*The undocumented witness of your existence unfolded
behind all the quiet bister mountains.*

*We use to sleep together on the shoulders of spring.
We use to communicate with quiet smiles on top of the
sierra. Now we dovetail with barren idioms as we sit
barely together in the middle of autumn.*

*The vestiges of our recollection are withering away swept
by the blue current that carries an early winter. Your
absence is shrouded in mortal ponds in whose
accidental moorings I barely stroll on.*

*The darkness is choking the light. The shadows are
sweeping in and I am washing my face in its stain.*

*I have subpoenaed my memory and only its consonants
are ready for me to peel their casings so I can write
on the leaves unglued from the frail branches.*

*Let's not get trapped in disjointed languishing dusks before
the flailing roots of deep winter deal its mistrustful
injustice, and the force of the
old rivers flood all winds forever putting them to the
gallows.*

The prologue to a requiem is being unleashed on this

naked good Earth!

I think I'll ride away with my soul on the wings of aboriginal feathers.

Shh... the shadows are still sleeping!

July 14, 2014.

A SCENT OF PERFUME – A DAY'S JOURNEY

I hiked the trails past broken serpentinous roads as a familiar scent emanated from the riverbanks of unplowed streams on my way toward the upper reaches of Mount Ungui.

A scent of isolation and curiosity led me to endless virginal valleys where they walked hand in hand with the mountain and seemed to walk alongside each other together.

I explored the lands once enriched by natives, past the willows, past the junipers, conifer and bamboo, while the swale invited me to its adaptive ways.

I unlocked and crossed the bridges of sunsets and clouds to become one with the root of the earth.

I penetrated the untraveled latitudinal slopes where the heart crawls at the speed of a passive stream.

The land invited me to become part of the earth. The soil that surrounded me was full of the tubers, as well as its Paleo-ecological diversification full of footprints of Violas, Spelitias and Ourisias.

Their scent seemed to fuse me to the whole of the clay by the rain in a form of Epiphytism.

I was walking towards the window where traces of forgotten lights were obliterated by the fog in my trail, as Incas provided me with company as well as guidance on my interminable road away from solitude and stillness.

I was on my way in the direction of my abode where my

inner consciousness cohabited with my soul weaving
moons on the sodden sloped grasses of my journey.

May 31, 1973- April 17, 2003.

IN THE EVENT

*How will you greet me in the event that I attend my own
funeral. It will not be a contradiction, nor out of the
ordinary for these events always happen in the
mind tales that perpetually parallel my abstract dreams.*

*I may no longer be able to be summoned to smile, nor to
play with the rain and ride on chariots with ghosts that
survived the last ice age.*

*As the outline of my voice excretes variations of breaths
instead of corresponding words, you and I will still be able
to dream and walk toward invented dreamt cities,
bastions of endless midnight chimeras.*

*The lid of my soul is raised toward the transparent light.
You will be able to discern its fingerprints before my last
abandonment of earthly years.*

*Faded shadows will follow and climbing in the direction of
indefinable living dreams where our lips will embrace each
other once more.*

*We will walk toward daylight where we will glance at each
other's heart and in an eternal extant communion for its
last journey where my bones will scrawl on papyrus!*

May 31 2011 – December 12, 2014

IN THE MUSEUM

*At the vortex of our memory, our remembrances queue on
the flowered wallpaper huddling as in an asylum of
multiple unfettered visions.*

*Behind the shadows, events march towards forests of rain
drops gasping, emulating seeds spreading themselves in a
corral hiding within rolling islands along the night valley.*

*Like tourists visiting the brain on precise highways, images
walk and lead to the gallery of germinating organic time
painting canvasses of a whirlwind eternity in
the form of a hieroglyph.*

*Our collection of history is exhibited as a collective of mind
ripples and specimens, illustrated on robes as a legacy to
our visions of song images.*

December 20, 1993.

MIGRANT

As a child I arrived in this land with more a sigh than a destination. I emigrated from historic Sierra de La Albera, its mountains resembled priests guarding the caged edges of the universe.

Accompanying my saintly Mother who came for life-serving surgery six years before, I arrived during the time when my dreams amalgamated with a Dadaist sunrise painted in purple, the same as my stone masoned terraced chimeras.

I left my childhood friends and classmates, arriving with a lavishly rich culture and language to share. I had an unwavering determination to survive, succeed, adapt and integrate, not to assimilate.

As time went by, I grew into an introspective and thoughtful Poet. I always felt I had arrived looking for a home in which I could swim and fish in your rivers, drink your waters, maybe even bathe myself in your flag.

*As soon as I became an independent thinking adult, the Vietnam War became an important issue.
I expressed those concerns to my classmates who had initially welcomed me with open arms. They rejected my opposition to the war with scorn.*

They fleered, reminding me that my ideas were acceptable only as long as they reflected and re-enforced the status quo and my lowly position; that of a brown intruder who had no right to any opinion.

They neglected to notice that my coagulated blood came

from the same quarry as all of us on the same planet and of the same destiny.

In spite of my reserve, I volunteered for the war for the country that I had adopted as my own. Speckles of glistening, quivering tears and sweat went into this decision, one that will haunt me for the rest of my life.

So here I am many years apart, in spite of the fact that I reminded my new countrymen that I migrated as we all migrate, as migrating birds have, other mammals, plants and even insects have done for millions of years. In fact it has been the defining trait of all living things. Indeed it has been encoded in our genes.

I am still a foreign brown enigma with only a trace of humanity. It seems my visible lament and conflicted varied rhythms still exasperates my brethren.

The indignity of my exiled migration has continued. They do not understand why I came, since there were no resources being depleted, no natural disasters, famine, floods or even war in my land.

Would that have made them happy or made me a more acceptable immigrant? Guess not, because now I am still isolated as an alien.

We are all a recurring historical and geographical accident, a dwindling voice that dares to cross bridges, rivers, and mountains searching for a peaceful home for our soul to rest on

We are all wasting debris in search of gardens of silence
that live on new lands in this universe.

All our spatial and funerial footprints are the same.
We all drink in the same rain!

October 26, 1992.

I ALMOST SAID GOODBYE

The sustaining illuminating nurturing thunder is quietly rummaging through my mind, as my memories of you are dripping from my brow.

Silence is marching away as in a procession journeying down the corridor of the now empty house without your soul toward eternal oblivion.

The tree's tear is bearing its painful fruit as our garden is being organically irrigated with blood from our broken heart.

Galloping past the bruised moonlights, your fading voice is howling out of its quivering dwelling before the unknown dreamless forests deep bush.

Three days later petals are been thrown in the direction of your fallen body. Its deafening echoes are harming my ears.

Your voice can no longer carry perfect pitch to sing the folk songs of your land and the soil from which you sprouted as an alien geyser.

You left as you came, an apparition from far beyond the Iberian as well as Arab lands that hold your simmering seeds still looking for a port of call.

Other echoes will have to quilt new filaments of sunrays, for the poetic eloquence imbedded in your DNA is now but a silent ancient stirring.

Barren silence is peddling strands of mournful quotes. Full passages of Victor Hugo's Les Miserables are being heard wandering down bottomless gorges repeating what you thought were life's sage lessons and mantras.

"There is nothing better than a dream to start and create a future." "Even the darkest night will end and the sun will rise." "For the weak, dreams are impossible; for the fainthearted, it is the unknown; but for the valiant it is the ideal"

I wanted to have the opportunity to say goodbye, but I guess you could not wait for me. Now we both have to live with that.

You departed from me as you did many times, surreptitiously and under the cloak of mid-afternoon. I hope that you relived our last conversation when I reiterated that you had a stormy, uneven but ultimately successful life. So for now don't be afraid to die.

You have already done the hardest part in this universe which is to live on Earth. The rest takes care of itself, as we are mere passengers on the train to our last terminal.

From where we will wander throughout eternity's cosmos! I yearn that wherever you are right now, you are still singing the anthems of our land. "Not being heard is no reason for silence"

I still hear your voice from inside a 'Vasija de Barro' where you now gently reside.

March 30, 1979 – March 26, 2017.

A HANDSHAKE WITH THE EARTH

Disguised as unconfirmed dust, we amble along in search of an endless postponement of the calling to inhabit unknown fields.

We march on fields of daffodils, along with grape hyacinths as well as crocus on this vast ever shrinking expanse of forged wished-for gardens in our oblique encapsulated view.

We are swarmed by whistles and blaring trumpets that pierce our encoded harmony with mistrustful falling spaces that arrive hidden behind ploughed fountains of lament inside our dreams.

They arrive after crossing bridges and logrolling over unused years where we were lured by cat's eyes from another creation that pantomimed what is, as of now, an un-engraved Earth.

We are indebted to extracted itinerant loves that move in and out incoherently along effluvium that leave winsomely brewed footprints.

With casual gratitude, we find ourselves shrugging as we finally amalgamate our age with a pre-determined destiny.

The light of the last lighthouse is whispering its deciduous whimpering silence!

January 21, 2015.

MY VOICE

*My voice is unraveling. My breath is turning to vapor
breaking certain provisions of history with it.*

*It is dematerializing itself, and in the process weaving
silence in shapes that visit white glaciers.*

*My voice melts and dances away towards abstract rivers
with profane primitive names that lie beyond
clouded enclosures.*

*They descend through undisclosed clenched dreams
whirling around blank unvisited quarries that populate our
imagination.*

*My utterances whisper their liquid tones to burgeoning
agile springs, as well as to my blinded eyes which went
into darkness as a result of a sharpened water branch
kidnapped out of a serene naked lake.*

*Bubbling spoonfuls of sound vibrate as they go through a
white doorway retreating... emulating the tides
of my voice's fate.*

*They are lurking and clutching onto the sweet water which
with its waves will take us for a stroll
over a sandy shore.*

*I think I'll go searching for the remnants of my voice before
it completely dissipates. Then it will no longer be able
to intone, mutter or murmur: I love you.*

April 01, 2015.

LET ME CRY ON YOUR SHOULDER

I want us to mourn in silence together while the oxygen in our dwelling is escaping down the railing in the middle of an injured autumn directly under the sepulchral riven in the sky that even Zeus cannot cover.

Please let me dream while I cry on your shoulder!

My beckoning desire is to be in love with the penumbra of your spirit which impregnates your existence.

I am in love, as well, with the glare of a painting in your eyes that reflect and capture the images through which you loiter, capturing scenes of the bliss of past dances.

Please let me dream while I cry on your shoulder!

I am jealous of the unlicensed air that you breathe and that flow through your being.

I am distrustful and resentful of the winds that caress you without my permission.

I am envious of the sun rays that warm your body and make you smile.

I am distrustful and resentful of the winds that caress you without my permission.

I am envious of the sun rays that warm your body and make you smile.

Please just let me dream...
I am in love with the hypnotic sway and command of your

sinuous waist which causes whitecaps that block the vista of the moon and horizon!

Please let me dream while I cry on your shoulder!

Please just let me dream...

I am in love with the hypnotic sway and command of your sinuous waist which causes whitecaps that block the vista of the moon and horizon!

Please let me dream while I cry on your shoulder!

You know that I worship and covet your Braquean structure that was born, conceived and engendered to spawn uninterrupted epistolary mystery and desire that inspire all of my natural senses.

Please let me dream why I cry on your shoulder!

Travel, glide and ride on the veins of my marrow as you visit these fiery byways. Please let me ensnare you with the net in my heart before I quietly depart permanently visit the faraway guestless heavens.

Please let me dream while I cry on your shoulder!

Take off your angel wings and land on the pores of my naked desire...but before you depart, leave a tattoo of your beautiful face in my bowels.

Please let me dream while I cry on your shoulder!

Today I thank the counterfeit god for creating you to be my singular moon and co-habit my dreams forever inspiring my wandering soul.

And as daylight gently limps and slips on charcoal into the night, before darkness lights its ominous enveloping pyre, please just let me dream and weep on your shoulder!

April 02, 2002

MIDNIGHT VOICES

Midnight voices are being reeled in, as the adroitly woven years dig in haunted gardens, looking for artifacts resting beneath invisible ruins of auroras rising over drunken landscapes.

The dead voices of the night are hanging on clothes lines that elicit mundane existences built on tiltyards filled with bodies of the forfeited lives of those not spoken about in the apostolic epistles.

Midnight voices are flocking towards hollow caverns to cohabit alongside orchards of suns sealing our vision of preceding generations made of gritty structures starving for Architecture within the crevices of empty time.

In nights bereft of oxygen, I explore through the knotted viaducts and mine shafts filled with deposits of frayed light rays leering at the last dust emanating from a rampike of rusted antediluvian time.

Don't grieve for the falling acorns as well as the yellow rain being harvested by my skin. They are mere reminders of life's continuum within the confines of celestial bodies masking condolences carried by astral floodwaters.

The sound of skipping stones over water are chiming in, whispering muted notes as spring surfaces along lonesome midnight balconies behind the dream slits of sunsets rippling in my heart.

The unfaithful moon's voice is sleeping with voyeur songs

giving birth in between the wrinkles of tides drawn out of myth and muzzled disenchantment riding on top of slithering mossy stones.

I am scouring for crocheted correspondence between the slashing images of midnight gardens and the frail absolved voices uttering uninhibited prayers and sermons devoid of transitional allegiance to our midnight howls.

November 28, 2010 - April 11, 2011.

TALES OF FAR AWAY MOONS

Secular serenity engulfs me as I voyage through the filled craters of the Earth rummaging through alien Easter Islands.

Moss is thriving under molten glass baked by echoes of unmoored treasures wearing far flung flesh tossing it to the winds to ride on air currents.

Rain is rocking my world braided in granite where eternal time travel blankets me with its discharging flash from far away moons.

Where are we going anyway?

June 01, 1983 – June 01, 2016.

MY TRUE ROOTS

I emerged from within the layers of a metamorphic stone that was hidden inside the silent shrubs in company of birds.

I emanated from the shadows long abandoned and forgotten in the mud.

I'm part of quiet histories that dissipate under the moss along with many queries.

I am a product of fermented dawns written in the liturgy when they were speaking of twilights and such hidden in the penumbra of almond trees.

I was born as a handiwork of tears that danced to the rhythm of lighting all dressed in golden tunics and conjured by long dead wizards of the dark.

I am but a seed in the sunset often confused with apocryphal howling before they were rescued by the light of day and watercolors hand painted in the water.

I originate directly from the native stone that mumbles in the night so as to converse with the mockingbirds.

August 22, 2003.

FROZEN

Frozen narratives raid the unhurried graves of the leaning
embalmed snowflakes as gales scatter and
disassemble them.

Usurped barren souls are being disinterred past cobwebs
of melancholy that encounter running across
lands with no name.

Life ebbs and collapses before our birth and turns into an
explosive muted cry.

Frozen detached fire is liberating us from our plasma...

The timid night prances on top of mountains of liquid
silence... before it freezes before our eyes.

The insurrected imagery's sunrays are slashing our
fragmented harmony in the middle of our maiden voyage.

We are being plucked away from this stammering Earth
toward forests of never ending hermetic stillness.

Nothing is naked before the light as a prologue to the end.

We are but a flat-line resting on the transparent
wrenching roots of our transcendent labyrinthian Earth!.

January 16, 2017.

IN ALCOVES OF SILENCE

*A lukewarm murmur welcomes me accompanied by a
bouquet of caresses, which until today had remained
bottled in alcoves of silence, walled by rivers woven and
quilted in silver by the eventful history of its
rugged orography.*

*Between fragments of forgotten petals, the inseparable
hearts that accompanied me more loved the flesh of a
destination more than the landscape of reality.*

*More to the smile and the twinkles of love than to the
profane thresholds that wallow in a garden of shadows.*

*I walk by forgotten furrows where the passions of love spill
in desired and painted abstract glaciers dancing over
borders that melt the lines of my youth.*

*Love and loneliness is like mythology; symbol of lies,
desires and myths*

*I wash my face with the darkness, and withdraw my name
and image from the obituary notice.*

*I would love to inherit the Earth before they cry for my
absence!*

December 31, 2007.

THE HUES OF MY LIFE

*The mistress of the angels arrived under the skirt of a mist
in a long un-begotten evening trying to un-chain itself
from the apocryphal blackness.*

*A suspicious field of stars was gathering in the once absent
fissure of the firmament carrying an array of shimmering
prophesies foretelling an emancipated silence...*

*Evanescent twinkling hearts were beating at the gates just
as I began to sail onward until my next stop in the stellar
system, deep into the white froth of the strings holding the
universe announcing my genesis.*

*The fading cliffs gathered together behind the twilight's
shadows. I was born under an embryonic spring that
seemed to reject me even before my face shone smiling
before this heavenly body.*

*Now my life is ebbing away behind the umbra of particles
and atoms in residence. My existence is drenched by grief
stricken rain which is wrecking my lair as it is gathers
spattered bleeding moss. It is time to move on.*

*The space rainbows and its rhythms are accosting me, so I
drink my leftover ailing youth in a chalice under
candlelight before it fades into darkness.*

*I am withdrawing to my interlude, to the eternal burning
light of the firmament... just under a wrinkle in the sun and
the dustpan of the universe.
Nothing but life is eternal!*

December 19, 2016.

SETTINGS

I feel my life ebbing not only through my pores, but by the rowels in my spurs. My decaying protoplasm no longer needs to pretend to know about its prearranged destiny.

I feel even the moon rays can't filter, subvert and quell the script. This life does not spare sorrows.

This setting is ushering audacious broadsided attacks on virginal bleached darkness. It seems my body and soul have ripened and are ready to drip, daub and carefully be painted into the arteries of this earth: the canvass of life and cot of supernatural un-born ruthless unfinished winters.

The red comet's gravitational pull is forcing the collapse of leaves to fall and adroitly sleep and storm my heart.

I am being coerced to ride on fragmented wheels that are dragging me to a blind date with my forebears.
I'm confused by the lost stolen alphabet in this translation.
I've turned into an expatriated ghost that lives and visit chapels of silence and shadows.

I am sparring with multiple ABC's that are turning into elusive smoke which is intermingling with haunted echoes of distant lands that lie amputated at the bottom of alluvial river beds hiding in my gaze.

The atoms are still percolating as I drink the notes of the awakened strands of a lush legacy as I walk on plains of clay

May 02, 1960 – April 17, 1982.

PORTALS

Through the long forgotten fenced in river portal, I enter your world in search of your eyes, nature's latticework in your cathedral.

Across savage two lane shadows and epic skeletons of electricity, I march through the shivering portals of nomadic time that meanders along the inroads of my legacy.

On my way toward you, fluid incantations flow, juggling past secret gypsy stones and the ebbs of tributaries wedding the seas in quarrel with our remains.

I've journeyed through awakenings littered with boughs, seeded and ensnared by measureless grief. Though gashed, I continue to ramble in search of truth's echoes hiding behind undiscovered shores.

I'm visiting forests of existence where you reside as a sapling leaping over ancient lathe turned pillars of salt oozing a diminishing penumbra to process my migrant dream. Let's go through the silk and almond portals of luscious Aphrodisia together.

Let's empower ourselves to cradle the last drops of time together... while we escape the hours huddled under the wounded and raw solitude of the last portal's vestibule.

Let's hold hands under the battling clouds yearning for fearless eternal peace and love, away from the water front's waterfront's rain and barefoot aurora.

January 01, 2017.

GALLOPING PAST TIME

*I gallop past the shadow-less tentacles of time embracing
the leather flame rising to pierce the riverboat's hull
floating on top of sweet water ponds along with
the birds of midnight.*

*The branches of my muted voyage have no memory, no
recall of the Earth beating though kaleidoscopic glass
harvesting the love along its vigil for freedom amid
wrinkled worn-out dreams.*

*Time was born under the naked light radiating from the
heart of melting clocks and hand painted rainbows
cantering on rivers of fire.*

*We stride past a world in quarrel with prolonged
intoxicating farewells, dismembered shadows as well as
the remains of the cries grazing over lost smuggled lands
living at the edges of non-inventoried penumbras.*

*The leaned seconds are accosting the nightingales' nests
and the songs flowing out of their throats, as I regurgitate
shattered water colored hunting queries.*

*The ripened enigmatic pre-ordained byways all sprout
moss, as caged ashes are disguised as imperishable
existence.*

*Musk vapors clothed in the radiant dawn of darkness are
now visible.*

Warp time is melting into the universe's paradox.

July 14, 2009.

AND THE RAINS KEPT COMING

As winter inexorably approached, it coincided with my mind attempting to reclaim its anachronistic symbol for lost silent strength, my knowing smile, wit and healthy moaning swagger.

As the wrinkled burning flames were being doused by the endless cold rain, the couriers of aging deposited sobering, bruising messages to my puzzled confused mind.

They undressed my bravado devoid of clarity and reality with pearls of humility. As the succession of interminable precipitation continued, my clumsy incompetent notions were abducted by reality.

Winter deals the growing season an urgent message. The drizzle sends the same subtle messages to my hurting, aching bones.

Only winter aconites are preparing to bloom through the rain and snow despite the decay around it.

I think I will accompany the birds in their travel to the southern hemisphere. Spring will come soon. Life continues onward in spite of the cold rain!

Spring brings forth the vernal equinox when the sun crosses horizons and as of yet unconquered benign lands holding hands with the sun heading north along the ecliptic.

The increasing daylight creates paths of eternal hope, blue birds, and compassionate embracing breezes. Flowers are blooming, and so is our eternal young heart.
In spite of the incessant rhythms of the cold rains, budding

and transforming-seeds of daffodils journey to rebirth
along with streams of harvesting nourishing
vivid wheels of light.

Life is reborn under the shadows of a flourishing cold rain.

October 09, 1988.

I CAN STILL HEAR THE DRUMBEAT

*The turbulent sacred soundtrack of my soul blossom under
my skin, as its history and perfume are being herded
through my youthful wounds.*

*The sound and all its stains are set aflame toward the
beams that hold the entrance to my soul carved by the
diligence of enslaved movements.*

*Drum notes dance away from the fluid skin membranes
parallel to my heartbeat. It crosses territories that were
discovered by the rising tide of sound that ring and
punctuate the overtones of the Earth.*

*Drum notes dance from prehistoric nuanced syncopated
mornings all the way to eminently quiet evenings filled
with sonorous, rumbling and eloquent quiet vibrations.*

I can still hear the drumbeat. I am still breathing freedom.

I am alive!

February 07, 2015.

TIDY METAPHORS

The sweat of my dreams fell into a fish bowl of an allegory previously filled by a generation of tears from writing.

In days gone by, this space was full of transparent terrestrial sins as well as sighs and voices that kept asking profound questions about certain theorems lost in an Arctic sea.

In a world full of turbulent destinies, our souls' horizons are marked by a prophetic fire at the same time a furtive destiny are lost inside indecipherable light's twilight.

The sweat of my dreams puts out fires in chambers with scriptures that plunder and loot our hearts and minds.

*The tumult of proscribed chaotic metaphors is using a crystal bowl as a manger for silence to rest in.
Is there a threshold of hope for us?*

The sweat of my dreams puts out fires looming magical horizons of nothingness!

My destiny is walking on a string that is holding the globe which resembles a fishbowl!

I am serving a life sentence on Earth's pale shadow behind history's flourishing hymns to inner most allegories.

Music is now shallower as we journey through our chaotic seasons losing our hearing as well as razing sight which now runs shoeless through forests on fire.

The distant echoes of our presence are being dwarfed by soaring cryptic quiet bird songs that are friends of crystalline waters where we navigate with our old souls in tow on their way to lingering inscribed dust.

Don't be ashamed to only be a vessel for misunderstood metaphors in transition.

May 01, 2016.

WHERE WILL YOU FIND ME
Directly inspired by Jorge Carrera Andrade's poem

When I am dead... where will you find me? Travel towards
latitude 41,23 north, 2.9 east where I was born...
Barcelona.
There...
look for a row of weeping willows.
Don't forget that.

As a gentle breeze gathers and tilts the leaves of the
highest tree, climb towards the sky,
to the very top of this tree – then,
when you no longer feel the roots – climb down...

And when the impression of the ribs of this tree will have
gathered as a tattoo close to your heart, you will have
found me!

Now you and I together will disguise ourselves as kites and
Snow Finches...

And fly away towards the skies of
Sierra de la Albera to live and repose to the end of time!

May 31, 2015.

www.ingramcontent.com/pod-product-compliance
Lightning Source LLC
Chambersburg PA
CBHW052201090426
42741CB00010B/2365